ALTERNATOR BOOKS™

# HARRIET TUBMAN

## ABOLITIONIST AND AMERICAN HERO

NIKI AHRENS

Lerner Publications ◆ Minneapolis

**For the fierce helpers**



Lerner Publications Company
An imprint of Lerner Publishing Group, Inc.
241 First Avenue North
Minneapolis, MN 55401 USA

For reading levels and more information, look up this title at www.lernerbooks.com.

Main body text set in Aptifer Sans LT Pro.
Typeface provided by Linotype AG.

**Library of Congress Cataloging-in-Publication Data**

Names: Ahrens, Niki, 1979– author.
Title: Harriet Tubman: abolitionist and American hero / Niki Ahrens.
Description: Minneapolis: Lerner Publications, 2022 | Series: Boss lady bios (alternator books) | Includes bibliographical references and index. | Audience: Ages 8–12 | Audience: Grades 4–6 | Summary: "After escaping the horrors of slavery, Harriet Tubman devoted her life to helping others secure their freedom. Learn about the brave abolitionist's secret rescue missions, her courageous service in the Civil War, and more"—Provided by publisher.
Identifiers: LCCN 2020021717 (print) | LCCN 2020021718 (ebook) | ISBN 9781728404578 (lib. bdg.) | ISBN 9781728417646 (eb pdf)
Subjects: LCSH: Tubman, Harriet, 1822–1913—Juvenile literature. | Slaves—United States—Biography—Juvenile literature. | African American women—Biography—Juvenile literature. | African Americans—Biography—Juvenile literature. | Underground Railroad—Juvenile literature.
Classification: LCC E444.T82 A66 2021 (print) | LCC E444.T82 (ebook) | DDC 306.3/62092 [B]—dc23

LC record available at https://lccn.loc.gov/2020021717
LC ebook record available at https://lccn.loc.gov/2020021718

Manufactured in the United States of America
1-48515-49029-3/10/2021

# TABLE OF CONTENTS

Harriet Tubman often traveled through woods at night to avoid capture.

# FIRST RESCUE

**HARRIET TUBMAN CROSSED OVER THE PENNSYLVANIA STATE LINE IN THE FALL OF 1849.** After braving a grueling and dangerous journey, she was finally free. In Pennsylvania, unlike Harriet's home state of Maryland, slavery was illegal. Freeing herself motivated Tubman to go back to rescue her loved ones. She was confident that she could lead them to safety.

With great courage, Tubman risked her freedom and her life to help others escape slavery. Returning to states where slavery was legal meant traveling swiftly in the dark of night. It meant making secret plans with trusted helpers along the route. With enslavers on the lookout for runaways, Tubman had to be acutely aware of her surroundings. But she was fiercely determined to lead others to freedom, and her first rescue was followed by many more. Tubman became an iconic leader for helping to free enslaved people.

Tubman (*far left*) with family and friends around 1887

Enslaved people in Beaufort, South Carolina, around 1862

CHAPTER 1

# A CHILDHOOD ENSLAVED

**HARRIET TUBMAN WAS BORN ARAMINTA ROSS TO PARENTS WHO WERE ENSLAVED.** Because birth records were not kept for the children of enslaved parents, Harriet's birthday is unknown. She was likely born in February or March of 1822 in Dorchester County, Maryland.

Enslavers forced enslaved people to perform labor such as cotton picking, as shown here.

Harriet's ancestors were captured and taken from their home in Africa. They were brought to America, like other enslaved people, in the hold of a ship. Enslaved Africans were bought by white enslavers who forced them to labor without pay. Enslaved people were treated as property by white enslavers. They did not have basic human rights, and many were abused and mistreated. Slavery was legal in many parts of the United States until 1865.

Harriet and her family were enslaved to the white Brodess family. Harriet, her siblings, and her mother, Rit, were all enslaved to Edward Brodess. Harriet's father, Ben, was enslaved to Brodess's stepfather, Anthony Thompson. Records suggest that Harriet was a middle child with eight siblings. From the time she was a young child, Harriet was hired out to do forced labor for other white people.

A plantation in South Carolina around 1862

Enslaved people near their home on a plantation

When Harriet was just five years old, she was sent away to take care of another family's baby. She looked after the baby all hours of the day and night. Harriet felt homesick when her enslaver rented her to others. She understood the injustices of slavery early on. Around the age of six, she ran away for five days after being caught tasting sugar and facing harsh punishment. Harriet only returned to her enslaver's farm because she was starving. Back at the farm, she was whipped.

Cruel conditions impacted Harriet's health. When she was around seven, she was sent into waist-deep wetlands to check muskrat traps. She had to continue working even while sick with the measles, and she became gravely ill. After she recovered, young Harriet was sent back to harsh work environments. Each year, her enslaver hired her out to different farms, separating her from her family. When she returned, she was often weak and sick. Beatings and whippings left permanent scars.

From a young age, Harriet was forced to do the kind of hard field labor shown here.

This hymnal, a book of religious songs, belonged to Tubman's great-niece.

By the age of twelve, Harriet had seen two of her sisters sold, and she was subjected to long, hard hours of work in the fields. Around this time, she received a severe head injury. An overseer threw an iron weight at an enslaved person and hit Harriet by accident. The injury afflicted Harriet with seizures and headaches for the rest of her life. At the same time, Harriet began to experience powerful images and dreams. The visions led her to become more devoted to her Christian faith, and she drew on them to direct the path of her life.

Enslaved people working in sweet potato fields around 1862

## CHAPTER 2
# FREEDOM FIGHTER

**HIRED OUT TO ANOTHER ENSLAVER, TEENAGE HARRIET LABORED IN THE FIELD AND THE WOODS, DOING WORK MORE COMMONLY DONE BY MEN WHO WERE ENSLAVED.** She grew strong from lifting, pulling, and chopping outdoors. She plowed fields and carried wood in a community of enslaved and free Black families. In 1844 she married freeman John Tubman, but she herself remained enslaved.

While logging and working the fields, Tubman became aware that enslaved people communicated with free people who wanted to help them. She observed a secret messaging chain between enslaved people living on plantations and free Black men working along the river and by the shipyards. They would pass messages by meeting in the forest under cover of night. Free Black men knew of safe places and helpers between the plantation and free states. Tubman thought this hidden network could help her gain the freedom she desired.

Tubman as a young woman

Fleeing enslavement was very dangerous. Few chose to take the risks. Most, instead, found other ways to resist.

Tubman was in her late twenties when she decided to risk her life to escape enslavement. Her husband refused to run away with her, but she was determined to have liberty. After an unsuccessful attempt with two of her brothers, she left again on her own. She turned north and set out for Pennsylvania, the nearest free state.

Tubman traveled one of the routes that became known as the Underground Railroad. These routes were neither underground nor a railroad. Instead, a secret network of thousands of people helped enslaved people find their way from one safe "station" to the next.

Examples of Underground Railroad routes between 1830 and 1865

A station might be a home, business, or other structure—anyplace where someone escaping slavery could seek shelter.

This Maryland house belonged to an abolitionist, who turned it into a stop along the Underground Railroad.

A group of people who escaped slavery outside a Virginia cabin in 1862

Tubman traveled at night, when it was easier to stay hidden. Sometimes she hid in a wagon, but she mainly moved on foot. Finally, she reached Pennsylvania. For the first time in her life, Tubman was free.

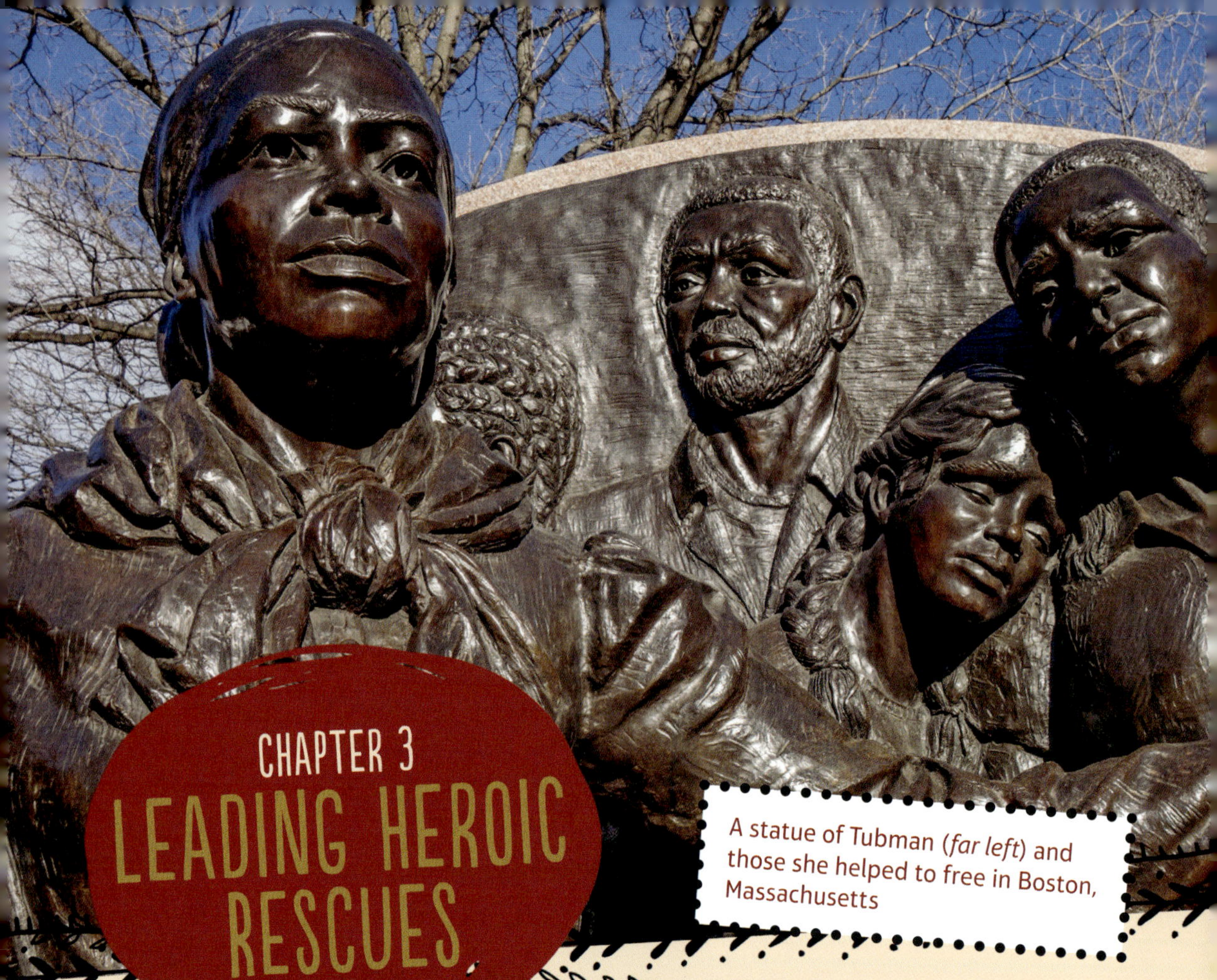

A statue of Tubman (*far left*) and those she helped to free in Boston, Massachusetts

CHAPTER 3

# LEADING HEROIC RESCUES

**ONCE TUBMAN EXPERIENCED FREEDOM, SHE WANTED HER FAMILY TO HAVE IT TOO.** Later, she described her loneliness: "There was no one to welcome me to the land of freedom. I was a stranger in a strange land." With exceptional courage, she went back to lead family members and other enslaved people along the Underground Railroad that she had traveled.

Her first return was for her niece Kessiah and Kessiah's two children. When Tubman learned that Kessiah was to be sold at an auction, Tubman acted immediately. Risking her newfound freedom, she planned a rescue to lead her niece's family to safety. Succeeding with this first rescue gave Tubman confidence in her skills.

Tubman kept traveling to rescue more enslaved people. She returned again for her brother and two of his acquaintances. Her third rescue freed eleven enslaved people, including strangers. Tubman helped so many people that she became known as the Moses of Her People, after the biblical hero who led enslaved Jewish people out of Egypt. Tubman's husband, John, had remarried and never joined her.

An illustration of Moses, to whom Tubman was often compared, freeing the Jewish people from slavery in Egypt

Over her many rescues, Tubman became a master of finding her way by reading natural signs.

Tubman gained a prominent role in the Underground Railroad. She became especially skilled at mass escapes. Tubman often used disguises or distracted enslavers and others who were trying to capture her. She always returned to the South alone and carried a pistol to protect herself and her northbound "passengers." A keen observer, Tubman found her way using clues in nature such as moss or algae, which often grew on the north side of trees. Tubman still experienced headaches and even seizures from her old injury. But she didn't let anything stop her from leading passengers to freedom.

"I WAS THE CONDUCTOR OF THE UNDERGROUND RAILROAD FOR EIGHT YEARS, AND I CAN SAY WHAT MOST CONDUCTORS CAN'T SAY—I NEVER RAN MY TRAIN OFF THE TRACK AND I NEVER LOST A PASSENGER."

Tubman led between thirteen and nineteen rescue trips, saving at least seventy and perhaps hundreds of enslaved people. In one of her final rescues, she led her parents, both in their seventies, to freedom.

An illustration of Tubman

Soldiers in the Union army in Virginia

CHAPTER 4

# BEYOND UNDERGROUND

**IN 1861 THE CIVIL WAR (1861–1865) STARTED BETWEEN THE UNION, OR THE UNITED STATES, AND THE CONFEDERACY, SEVEN STATES THAT SEPARATED FROM THE UNION TO KEEP SLAVERY.** Harriet Tubman aided the Union army in the war. In her new role, Tubman led efforts to get needed supplies and training to Union soldiers and helped to nurse the sick and wounded. She also helped those who'd just escaped slavery begin to build new lives. She organized paid work for newly free women in Union army camps. Tubman eventually became a spy for the Union army and even led soldiers in a raid. Her leadership freed more than 750 enslaved people. The war ended in 1865, and legal slavery was abolished except for as punishment for a crime.

An illustration of the Battle of Fredericksburg in 1862

*From left:* Tubman; her adopted daughter, Gertie; and her husband Nelson Davis around 1887

Although slavery had mostly ended, racism hadn't. Tubman was a war hero, but she wasn't paid for most of the work she did, and she continued to face unfair treatment. While some war veterans received monthly payments from the government, Tubman did not. She married a former soldier named Nelson Davis in 1869, and they adopted a daughter named Gertie in 1874. Tubman and Davis tended a farm together, but they struggled with poverty and hunger. Davis died in 1888.

In her sixties, Tubman continued to fight for causes that mattered to her. She advocated for women's rights. She focused on the rights of Black women, who had been largely left out of the women's suffrage movement. Tubman also raised funds and opened a home for the poor and elderly. When she was seventy-seven, she finally began to receive a payment of twenty dollars per month for her military service and her status as a soldier's widow. She died on March 10, 1913.

Tubman's house in Auburn, New York, where she spent her last years

"IF YOU ARE TIRED, KEEP GOING; IF YOU ARE SCARED, KEEP GOING; IF YOU ARE HUNGRY, KEEP GOING; IF YOU WANT TO TASTE FREEDOM, KEEP GOING."

Throughout her life, Tubman never gave up the struggle for racial justice. With challenges and obstacles in her path, she kept going and never lost her way.

Harriet Tubman

# RESISTING SLAVERY

History books and media often highlight stories of enslaved people who escaped. But trying to escape was both difficult and dangerous. Enslaved people risked their health and their lives. Few succeeded in reaching freedom.

Most enslaved people didn't try to escape. They found different ways to resist. Some people broke tools, faked illness, or set fires to slow down or stop work. Others refused to use names enslavers had given them. Some organized revolts against enslavers. Enslaved people also worked to keep the cultures and histories of their homelands alive.

Harriet Tubman is an example of extraordinary courage in her resistance to slavery. All forms of resistance worked against and undermined the unjust institution of slavery in the US.

# TIMELINE

1822 Araminta Ross is born into slavery in Maryland.

1844 Ross marries freeman John Tubman and begins to call herself Harriet Tubman.

1849 Tubman escapes slavery and finds freedom in the state of Pennsylvania, where slavery is illegal.

1851 Tubman begins leading enslaved people to freedom along the secret Underground Railroad.

1861 Tubman works as a nurse, scout, and spy for the Union army and leads a raid to free more than 750 enslaved people.

1896 Tubman purchases land for a home for the ill and elderly.

1913 Tubman dies and receives military honors at her burial.

2015 The US Treasury announces plans to feature Tubman on the twenty-dollar bill.

2021 After a hiatus, the US Treasury resumes plans to put Tubman on the twenty-dollar bill.

# GLOSSARY

**abolish:** to end or do away with something completely

**advocate:** to actively support a cause that one favors

**ancestor:** a person that someone is descended from

**enslavement:** the holding of people as owned property

**enslaver:** someone who buys, sells, or owns enslaved people

**free state:** a US state in which slavery was illegal before the Civil War

**justice:** a state of fair rights and laws

**labor:** work

**overseer:** an enslaver who supervised enslaved people while they worked

**plantation:** a large farm or estate where many laborers grow crops or maintain land

**seizure:** a sudden change in the brain's electrical activity, often resulting in loss of consciousness

**suffrage:** the right to vote

# SOURCE NOTES


18 Erica Armstrong Dunbar, *She Came to Slay: The Life and Times of Harriet Tubman* (New York: Simon & Schuster, 2019), 39.

21 Dunbar, 138.

26 Laurie Calkhoven, *Harriet Tubman: Leading the Way to Freedom* (New York: Sterling, 2008), 1.

# LEARN MORE

Agard, Sandra A. *Harriet Tubman: A Journey to Freedom.* New York: Random House, 2019.

America's Story from America's Library: Harriet Tubman http://www.americaslibrary.gov/aa/tubman/aa_tubman_subj.html

Britannica: Harriet Tubman https://www.britannica.com/biography/Harriet-Tubman

Cline-Ransome, Lesa. *Before She Was Harriet.* New York: Holiday House, 2018.

deRubertis, Barbara. *Let's Celebrate Emancipation Day & Juneteenth.* New York: Kane, 2018.

Kiddle: Harriet Tubman Facts for Kids https://kids.kiddle.co/Harriet_Tubman

McDonough, Yona Zeldis. *Who Was Harriet Tubman?* New York: Penguin Workshop, 2019.

National Park Service: Harriet Tubman https://www.nps.gov/people/harriet-tubman.htm

# INDEX



# PHOTO ACKNOWLEDGMENTS

Image credits: Boris Ryaposov/Shutterstock.com, p. 4; Wikimedia Commons (public domain), pp. 5, 15; Library of Congress (LC-DIG-cwpb-00735), p. 6; Library of Congress (LC-DIG-stereo-1s02973), p. 7; Library of Congress (LC-DIG-stereo-1s04463), p. 8; Library of Congress (LC-DIG-stereo-1s03956), p. 9; Library of Congress (LC-DIG-ppmsca-39592), p. 10; Collection of the Smithsonian National Museum of African American History and Culture, Gift of Charles L. Blockson, pp. 11, 24; Library of Congress (LC-DIG-ppmsca-11398), p. 12; Benjamin F. Powelson/Wikimedia Commons (public domain), p. 13; Everett Collection/Shutterstock.com, p. 14; Jerrye & Roy Klotz, MD/Wikimedia Commons (CC BY-SA 3.0), p. 16; Library of Congress (LC-DIG-cwpb-01005), p. 17; Heidi Besen/Shutterstock.com, p. 18; Providence Lithograph Company/Wikimedia Commons (public domain), p. 19; photolike/Shutterstock.com, p. 20; National Portrait Gallery, Smithsonian Institution, p. 21; Library of Congress (LC-DIG-ppmsca-34548), p. 22; Library of Congress (LC-DIG-ds-07454), p. 23; Randy Duchaine/ Alamy Stock Photo, p. 25; Collection of the National Museum of African American History and Culture shared with the Library of Congress, p. 26. Design element: kondratya/iStock/Getty Images (handwritten grunge font).

Cover: National Portrait Gallery, Smithsonian Institution.